Contents

UK

116 123 - Samaritans

0800 068 4141 - HopeLine UK

New Zealand

09 5222 999 (Auckland) – Lifeline New Zealand
0800 543 354 (Rest of NZ) - Lifeline New Zealand

France (English Speaking)

0033 145 39 4000 - Suicide Ecoute

01 46 21 46 46 - SOS Help

South Africa

0861 322 322 - Lifeline Southern Africa

Japan

Befrienders International, Tokyo - +81 (0) 3 5286 9090

BI Suicide Prevention Centre, Osaka - +81 (0) 6 4395 4343

Tokyo English Lifeline - 107-0062

Germany

Telefonseelsorge Deutschland (National)

German speaking: 0800 -111 0 222

English speaking: 030-44 01 06 07

What is generalised anxiety disorder (GAD)?

GAD is a long-term condition that causes an individual to feel anxious about a wide range of situations and issues, rather than one specific event.

Most individuals will experience anxiety, a feeling of unease, worry or fear. This can be mild or severe.

Every individual has feelings of anxiety from time to time, such as feelings of worry before getting married or sitting an exam.

During these situations, feeling anxious is perfectly normal.

However some individuals find it hard to control their worries. This anxiety is more constant and often will affect their day to day lives.

People with GAD feel anxious most days and often struggle to remember the last time they felt relaxed.

As soon as one anxious thought is resolved, another may appear about a different issue.

Symptoms of GAD and when to get help

GAD can cause both psychological and physical symptoms.

These vary from individual to individual, but can include:

- feeling restless or worried
- having trouble concentrating or sleeping
- dizziness or heart palpitations

Although feelings of anxiety at certain times such as before a job interview are

completely normal, an individual should
see a doctor if the anxiety is affecting
their daily life or causing them distress.

GAD poem

I can't rest, I can't eat, I'm on the edge of my seat. I feel like I just can't cope, it's like there is a snake around my chest, I can't take a breath. Can I please swap this worry for hope?

Why GAD has physical symptoms

Listed below are some possible physical symptoms of anxiety

- stomach pain, nausea, or digestive trouble
- headache
- insomnia or other sleep issues
- weakness or fatigue
- rapid breathing or shortness of breath
- pounding heart or increased heart rate
- sweating
- trembling or shaking
- muscle tension or pain

Anxiety is the body's response to stress. When individuals feel emotionally stressed their bodies release hormones called adrenaline and cortisol. This is the body's way of preparing to respond to a threat, also known as the fight or flight response.

When the body responds to danger, an individual will breathe rapidly due to the lungs trying to move more oxygen through the body in case you have a need to escape. This can make an individual feel as if they're not getting enough air, which in turn could trigger further anxiety or panic.

The human body isn't meant to always be on high alert. Constantly being in fight or flight mode can have serious negative effects on an individual's body.

Muscles that are tensed may prepare an individual to get away from danger quickly, but muscles that are constantly tense can result in pain, tension headaches, and migraines.

If an individual if regularly stressed or anxious, frequently releasing these hormones can have long-term health effects. Your digestion may also change in response.

GAD in children

All children and teens have some form of anxiety. It's a normal part of development. However these worries and fears don't go away and may interfere with a child's normal activities.

Unlike adults with GAD, children and teens often don't realize that their anxiety is more intense than the situation calls for. Children and teens with GAD often need a lot of reassurance from the adults in their life.

Symptoms vary for each individual child but the most common symptoms are:

- Many worries about things before they happen

- Many worries about friends, school, or activities
- Almost constant thoughts and fears about the child's safety or the parents' safety
- Refusing to go to school
- Frequent stomachaches, headaches, or other physical complaints
- Muscle aches or tension
- Sleep problems
- Lots of worry about sleeping away from home
- Clingy behaviour with family members
- Feeling as though there is a lump in the throat
- Extreme tiredness
- Lack of concentration
- Being easily startled
- Being grouchy or irritated

Other problems

Anxiety is the main symptom of several other conditions conditions; this could mean that an individual has a different diagnosis other than GAD. Such as some of the conditions listed below:

- panic disorder
- phobias
- post-traumatic stress disorder (PTSD)
- social anxiety disorder (social phobia)

Possible causes of GAD

A specific cause of GAD is not fully known, however it is likely that a combination of multiple factors play a role. It is suggested that some of these factors could be:

- An over activity in areas of the brain involved in emotions and behaviour
- An imbalance of an individual's brain chemicals serotonin and noradrenaline, these are involved in the control and regulation of mood
- Inherited genes. An individual is estimated to be 5 times more likely

- to develop GAD if they have a close relative with the condition
- Having a history of stressful or traumatic experiences, such as domestic violence, child abuse or bullying
- Having a painful long-term health condition
- Having a history of substance abuse

However many individuals seem to develop GAD for no apparent reason.

Treatment

GAD can have an extremely large impact on an individual's daily life. Luckily there are several different treatments available that can ease symptoms such as:

- **psychological therapies** e.g. cognitive behavioural therapy
- **medicine** e.g. selective serotonin reuptake inhibitors (SSRIs)

With treatment, a lot of individuals are able to control their anxiety levels. However some treatments might need to be continued for a long period of time and there may be periods when symptoms get worse.

Accessing treatment

Listed below are some ways you could access treatment:

- **See your GP**

- **Free NHS therapy services**. If you live in the United Kingdom you can search for Improving Access to Psychological Therapies (IAPT) services in your area on the NHS website.

- **Specialist organisations**

- **Private therapists**.

Self help

There are many things an individual can do to help reduce anxiety, things like:

- enrolling on self-help course
- exercising regularly
- lowering alcohol and caffeine consumption levels
- downloading a GAD self help app

All of these points are a step in the right direction to help cope and control GAD.

Physical health

Looking after your physical health is paramount and makes a massive difference in how you feel emotionally. It can be extremely tiring to cope with GAD and it may feel like there is no energy left to take care of yourself but physical health is key in mental health.

Exercise - It can be extremely helpful for an individual's mental health and wellbeing to exercise. Through exercise an individual can set targets and positively gain a sense of achievement and take pride in what they are doing. Keeping active also helps individuals sleep by making them more tired at the end of the day. It manages stress and creates positive moods by releasing hormones into the body that make you feel better in yourself.

Diet - Eating regularly, choosing foods that release energy slowly and taking in enough water is a staple in mental health as it helps individuals to think more clearly and boosts energy

 If an individual's blood sugar drops that may leave them feeling tired and irritable so eating regularly and choosing foods that slowly release energy will help to keep sugar level stable.

Keeping hydrated is also very important as dehydration may leave you struggling to think clearly and creating headaches.

Keeping your gut happy because your gut can reflect your emotional state, for example if you are feeling anxious or stressed this can make your gut slow down. Fibre, fluids and regularly exercise helps to aid healthy digestion.

Nature – It may be a struggle for individuals to deal with the outside world but spending time with nature is an excellent way to boost wellbeing. Growing your own foods or flowers or spending time with animals can give an individual a sense of purpose, creates new connections and creates relaxation. This can help reduce feelings of anger and stress and improve an individual's mood and confidence.

Andy's story

From a very young age Andy was always known as a shy boy, he was scared of strangers, easily startled and always clung very tightly to his father's leg. "Scared of his own shadow" people would say.

Andy's parents just thought that he was a shy, nervous child and that was that.

Andy would panic whenever his parents left the house, gasping for air in a panic filled episode. This also happened whenever it was time for school, Andy would refuse to go and another panic filled episode would start.

Andy didn't really eat all that much. His parents thought that was the reason why he was extremely tired a lot and was struggling to concentrate at school. Andy would complain about stomach aches and muscle aches a lot too. Andy's parents always tried to make sure that he was eating enough.

He struggled to sleep or even to relax for that matter. He seemed very irritable.

Andy would always seem to be filled with anxiety with future events and what could happen.

Andy was 7 years old when his parents started to suspect that he was not just a shy nervous child. Andy's parents wanted to help their son and took him to the doctor's for some advice.

Whilst at the doctor's Andy clung tightly to his parents, breathing heavily and sweating prolifically.

His parents explained to the doctor that Andy was always a shy child and that they were worried that Andy was going to live his life in fear. The doctor reassured Andy and his parents and proceeded to ask some questions.

The doctor asked Andy if he ever got stomach aches or headaches from all his worry, Andy nodded his head. He was too scared to talk or even to look at the doctor. The doctor asked Andy's parents "Has there been any trauma in Andy's life such as a car accident or a home robbery and how well is he eating?", "Not nothing like and his eating is not so good" Andy's mother replied. Andy's mother was rubbing Andy's arm and this soothed him, the calm in the doctor's office helped Andy even though his anxiety was almost bringing him to tears. "How do you feel whenever your mother or father leaves you?" the doctor asked Andy. Andy is shaking and begins to sob, "I'm scared in case they get hurt and die and I never get to see them again" he replies in a whisper. "And do you always feel this worried about things?" the doctor asked. Andy replied with a tear filled "uh huh".

The doctor reassured Andy and his parents that there was help available. He informed them that he believed Andy was suffering from a generalised anxiety disorder and handed them some leaflets along with an offer to refer him for cognitive behavioural therapy.

Andy's parents graciously accepted this offer. Andy started to panic. He didn't like the sound of counselling, his breathing was rapid and his hands were flailing around him. The doctor quickly informed Andy and his parents that if he isn't comfortable yet with that option, there are plenty of other forms of help in the leaflets he had given. This information calmed Andy down even though he was still in panic mode.

Back at home and Andy and his parents sat down and looked in the leaflet. They found some ideas that sounded fantastic and Andy agreed. They sat and taught Andy how to take 3 deep breaths whenever he felt like he was getting too worried and then got out some arts and crafts and created a worry box out of an old tissue box and decorated it with all bright colours.

This worry box was so that every time Andy had a worry he could write it down on some paper and place it in the box. All of the support from his parents really helped Andy.

Andy still gets uncontrollable feelings of anxiety but he now knows how to manage it.

GAD poem

My stomach in knots and feet are so sore from the constant clench of anxiety. It seems all the time the weight on my mind is crushing me in my entirety.

References

- https://www.nhs.uk/mental-health/conditions/generalised-anxiety-disorder/overview/

- Raypole, C. (2019). *Physical Symptoms of Anxiety: How Does It Feel?* [online] Healthline. Available at: https://www.healthline.com/health/physical-symptoms-of-anxiety#symptoms.

- Rochester.edu. (2019). *Generalized Anxiety Disorder (GAD) in Children and Teens - Health Encyclopedia - University of Rochester Medical Center.* [online] Available at: https://www.urmc.rochester.edu/encyclopedia/content.aspx?ContentTypeID=90&ContentID=P02565.

Personal notes:

www.ingramcontent.com/pod-product-compliance
Lightning Source LLC
Chambersburg PA
CBHW070104260726

48658CB00002B/984